Read-About® Holidays

Chinese New Year

By David F. Marx

Consultants
Nanci R. Vargus, Ed.D.
Primary Multiage Teacher
Decatur Township Schools, Indianapolis, Indiana

Katharine A. Kane, Reading Specialist
Former Language Arts Coordinator,
San Diego County Office of Education

Children's Press®
A Division of Scholastic Inc.
New York   Toronto   London   Auckland   Sydney
Mexico City   New Delhi   Hong Kong
Danbury, Connecticut

Designer: Herman Adler Design
Photo Researcher: Caroline Anderson
The photo on the cover shows children participating in a Chinese
New Year celebration.

Library of Congress Cataloging-in-Publication Data

Marx, David F.
    Chinese New Year / by David F. Marx.
      p. cm. — (Rookie read-about holidays)
    Includes index.
    Summary: A simple introduction to the traditions and festivities of
Chinese New Year.
    ISBN 0-516-22267-8 (lib. bdg.)   0-516-27375-2 (pbk.)
    1. Chinese New Year—Juvenile literature. 2. Chinese—Social life
and customs—Juvenile literature. [1. Chinese New Year. 2. Holidays.]
I. Title. II. Series.
GT4905.M36   2001
394.261—dc21

                          2001028912

CHILDREN'S PRESS, and ROOKIE READ-ABOUT®,
and associated logos are trademarks and or registered trademarks
of Scholastic Library Publishing. SCHOLASTIC and associated logos
are trademarks and or registered trademarks of Scholastic Inc.
13 14 15 16 17 18 19 R 12 11 10   62

Open the doors and windows.
It's Chinese New Year!

China is a large country in Asia. It is on the other side of the world from North America. China has its own, special New Year's holiday.

January 2011

Sunday	Monday	Tuesday	Wednesday	Thursday	Friday	Saturday
						1
2	3	4	5	6	7	8
9	10	11	12	13	14	15
16	17	18	19	20	21	22
23	24	25	26	27	28	29
30	31					

Chinese New Year lasts
two weeks. It happens
in January or February.

February 2011

Sunday	Monday	Tuesday	Wednesday	Thursday	Friday	Saturday
		1	2	3	4	5
6	7	8	9	10	11	12
13	14	15	16	17	18	19
20	21	22	23	24	25	26
27	28					

8

Families clean their houses before the new year. They decorate their homes with flowers.

It is good luck if a flower blooms in your house on New Year's Day!

The holiday starts on New Year's Eve. Families come together for a big dinner.

11

Some families set extra places at the dinner table. These places are for missing family members. These people may be away from home, or may have died.

At midnight on New Year's Eve, people open their doors and windows. This lets the old year out and welcomes in the new year.

People also set off firecrackers. The firecrackers make a loud bang.

On New Year's Day, there are festivals in every Chinese community.

17

18

Groups of people dress up
in long dragon costumes and
dance through the streets.

One special day during
the two-week celebration
is for married women.
They travel back home
to visit the family they
grew up with.

People spend a lot of time
visiting friends during
Chinese New Year.
They bring oranges
and tangerines as gifts.

This tray of dried fruit has been left out for the new year celebration.

Chinese New Year ends with the Lantern Festival.

People make the lanterns themselves.

Fireworks light up the sky, too. What a beautiful, colorful way to welcome the new year!

Words You Know

door

dragon

festival

firecrackers

fireworks

flowers

lantern

oranges

Index

About the Author

David F. Marx is an author and editor of children's books. He resides in the Chicago area.

Photo Credits

Photographs © 2002: AP/Wide World Photos/Greg Baker: 4; Archive Photos/Getty Images/Larry Chan/Reuters: 29, 31 top left; China Stock: 27, 31 bottom left (Dennis Cox), 11 (Christopher Liu); Envision/Steve Needham: 25; James Levin: 21; Network Aspen: 17, 30 bottom left (Jeffrey Aaronson), 15, 30 bottom right (Phil Schermeister); Photo Researchers, NY/Lawrence Migdale: 12, 22, 31 bottom right; PhotoEdit: 26 (A. Ramey), 18, 30 top right (David Young-Wolff); Stock Boston: 8, 31 top right (Brent Jones), 3, 30 top left (Keren Su); Stone/Getty Images/Billy Hustace: cover.